The
Oxford Picture Dictionary
for Kids

Joan Ross Keyes
Illustrated by Sally Springer

OXFORD UNIVERSITY PRESS

Great Clarendon Street, Oxford OX2 6DP

Oxford University Press is a department of the University of Oxford.
It furthers the University's objective of excellence in research, scholarship,
and education by publishing worldwide in

Oxford   New York

Auckland   Cape Town   Dar es Salaam   Hong Kong   Karachi
Kuala Lumpur   Madrid   Melbourne   Mexico City   Nairobi
New Delhi   Shanghai   Taipei   Toronto

With offices in

Argentina   Austria   Brazil   Chile   Czech Republic   France   Greece
Guatemala   Hungary   Italy   Japan   South Korea   Poland   Portugal
Singapore   Switzerland   Thailand   Turkey   Ukraine   Vietnam

Oxford is a registered trade mark of Oxford University Press
in the UK and in certain other countries

ISBN 0 19-434996-9 (hardcover)
ISBN 0 19-434997-7 (softcover)

Copyright © 1998 Oxford University Press

Editorial Manager: Shelagh Speers
Senior Editor: June Schwartz
Editor: Dorothy Bukantz
Production Editor: M. Long
Elementary Design Manager: Doris Chen
Designer: David Hildebrand
Art Buyer: Donna Goldberg
Production Manager: Abram Hall

Printing (last digit): 10 9 8 7 6 5

Printed in Hong Kong.

Cover illustration by Sally Springer
Illustrations by Sally Springer
Cover design by Doris Chen

Additional art by: Gary Torrisi; Robert Frank/Melissa Turk & The Artist
Network; Marcia Hartsock, CMI; Elizabeth Wolf/Melissa Turk & The Artist
Network; Andrea Tachiera; Stephen Nicodemus; and John Paul Genzo.

Acknowledgements

To all my students everywhere whose appreciation and enthusiasm motivated me to create this book, its stories, dialogues,
and Beats!

To the special people at Oxford University Press: the design and production staff for ingeniously putting all the parts together, to
Shelagh Speers, the Editorial Manager, for her "go for it" encouragement, and most of all to my own editor, June Schwartz, whose
patient labors got us through it all.

And to my family, my daughter and three sons, for understanding and giving me space...

I thank you all.

JRK

Preface

The **Oxford Picture Dictionary for Kids** is designed especially for young students, ages five to seven, who are learning English.

The dictionary presents over 700 words in the context of pictures that tell stories. Five characters and their families are introduced at the beginning of the book, and appear throughout in 60 double-page illustrations.

Dictionary Organization

Each double-page illustration introduces a topic. The 60 topics are organized into nine themes. The initial focus is on the individual characters' experiences within the family, at home, and at school. The focus then expands to include their experiences in the neighborhood, around the town, and in other environments in the United States and around the world. Although the topics follow a logical progression, each topic is self-contained so that they may be presented to students in any order.

Under the double-page illustration in each topic are words and pictures corresponding to the objects or actions shown in that illustration. Each word is accompanied by a small picture that duplicates the item in the larger illustration. These *callouts* define the words. They help children isolate each item and search for it in the context of the picture story.

Each topic has 12 numbered callouts. In addition to the callout vocabulary, some pages have labels, such as for rooms in the house and in the school. The number of words has been kept to a minimum so that students will be able to master the vocabulary more easily. Verbs and nouns are included in topics together to encourage students to use the language in context. Verbs are grouped together on the page. Each verb is marked with a star.

Appendix and Word Lists

Following the 60 topics is an appendix that includes the alphabet, numbers, colors, shapes, days, months, and time.

After the appendix are three lists: *Words, Verbs,* and *Subjects.* The *Words* list, arranged alphabetically, includes the callout nouns and verbs, labels, and key words from the titles. These are listed in black. Listed in red are additional words that do not appear in the text, but are pictured in the illustrations.

The *Verbs* list is arranged by the topics in which verbs can be found.

The *Subjects* list is a convenient cross-reference, by category, of words that can be found within several different topics and themes.

Using the Dictionary as a Program

The dictionary can be used by itself or with other components that make it suitable as the core of an entire English-language curriculum. These components include the *Teacher's Book, Reproducibles Collection, Workbook, Cassettes,* and *Wall Charts.*

The Reproducibles Collection is a boxed set of four books of reproducible pages: *Word and Picture Cards, Stories, Beats!,* and *Worksheets.* The *Stories* describe each illustration; the *Beats!* are playful rhythmic chants for each topic. In the *Stories* and *Beats!* books, each illustrated sheet folds to make a mini-book for students to take home.

The *Teacher's Book,* in addition to complete notes for every topic, contains annotated bibliographies of appropriate theme-related literature to help create a classroom library.

The *Picture Dictionary* is available in both monolingual and bilingual editions.

Contents

Theme 4: My Town

Theme 5: Weekend

Theme 6: Vacation

Me

Tommy

Ting

Alison

Diego

Zoe

My family

The Matthews family

The Cheng family

The Young family

1. sister

2.  brother

3.  mother

4. father

5. parents

6. children

The Lopez family

The Jackson family

7. grandmother

8. grandfather

9. aunt

10.  uncle

11.  cousins

12. baby

Different faces

1.  eyes

2.  ears

3. nose

4.  mouth

5. 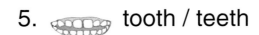 tooth / teeth

6.  chin

7. eyelashes

8. skin

9. hair

10. straight

11. curly

12. glasses

Europe

Asia

Africa

Australia

N
W E
S

Antarctica

Where do you live?

1. house

2. apartment

3. hill

4. street

5. address

6. telephone

7.  window

8. door

9. roof

10. tree

11. yard

12. fence

Good morning!

bedroom

bathroom

living room

1. stove

2. table

3. sink

4. dresser

5. bed

6. sofa

bedroom

kitchen

☆7. cook

☆8. eat

☆9. wash

☆10. brush

☆11. get dressed

☆12. sleep

Busy bathroom!

1. water

2. brush

3. comb

4. bathtub

5. shower

6. toothbrush

7. toothpaste

8. shampoo

9. soap

10. towel

11. toilet

12. toilet paper

1. sweater

2. underwear

3. sneakers

4. socks

5. baseball cap

6. dress

7. skirt

8. sweatshirt

9. jeans

10. T-shirt

11. boots

12. pajamas

Who made breakfast?

1.  bowl

2.  plate

3. cup

4.  glass

5. knife

6.  fork

7. spoon

8. juice

9. butter

10. cereal

11. eggs

12. bread

1. bus stop

2. bus driver

3. corner

4. line

5. seat

6. seat belt

7. lunch box

8. backpack

☆9. lean

☆10. push

☆11. stand

☆12. sit

Time for school

classroom

office

1. teacher

2. principal

3. nurse

4. student

5. crossing guard

6. librarian

library

art room

music room

nurse's office

cafeteria

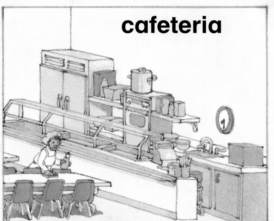

gym

7. car

8.  bicycle

9. bus

10. clock

☆11. walk

☆12. ride

1. picture

2. markers

3. pencil

4. crayons

5. scissors

6. glue

7. blocks

☆8. build

☆9. listen

☆10. look

☆11. paint

☆12. cut

1. book

2. notebook

3. paper

4.  board

5. desk

6. chair

7. chalk

8. wastebasket

☆9. write

☆10. draw

☆11. read

☆12. think

Bodies and bones!

1. head

2. neck

3.  chest

4. stomach

5. back

6. buttocks

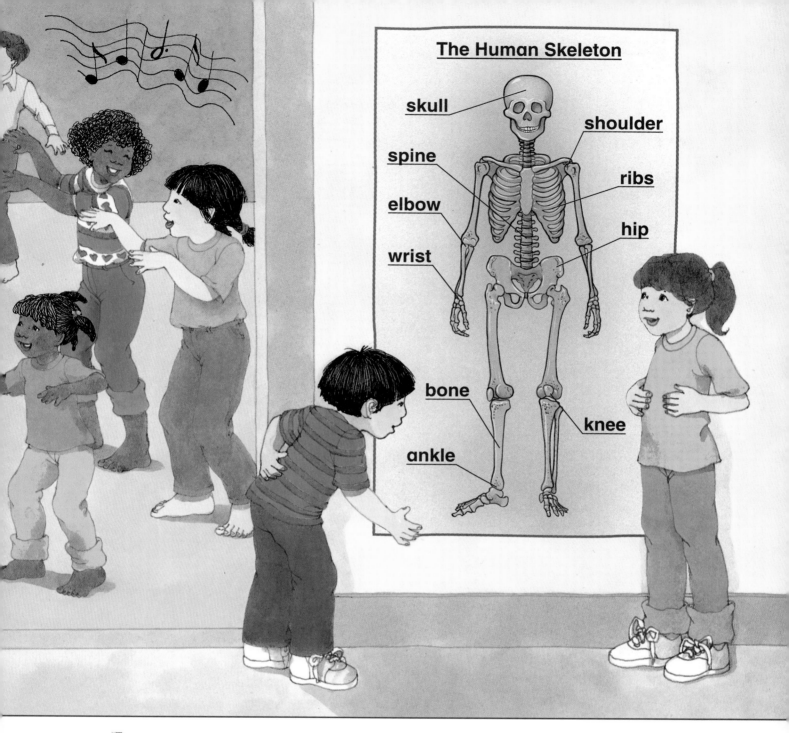

The Human Skeleton

skull

shoulder

spine

ribs

elbow

hip

wrist

bone

knee

ankle

7. leg

8. foot / feet

9. toes

10. arm

11. hand

12. fingers

What's new in the hall?

1. happy

2. sad

3. tired

4. surprised

5. angry

6. scared

7. worried

☆8.  smile

☆9. yawn

☆10. cry

☆11. frown

☆12. laugh

Gym time!

1.  hoop

2. 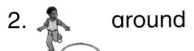 around

3.  between

4. over

5.  through

6.  under

7. mat

☆8. skip

☆9. hop

☆10. crawl

☆11. jump

☆12. tumble

What's for lunch?

1. tray

2. taco

3. apple

4. milk

5. can

6. carrot

7.  egg roll

8. sushi

9. garbage can

10. sandwich

11. salad

12. cookie

Let's play!

1. swing

2. slide

3. bars

4. seesaw

5. ball

☆6. climb

 7. throw

 8. catch

9.  bounce

 10. fall

11. run

12.  kick

What's the matter?

1. stomachache

2.  tissues

3. sore throat

4. fever

5. thermometer

6. bandage

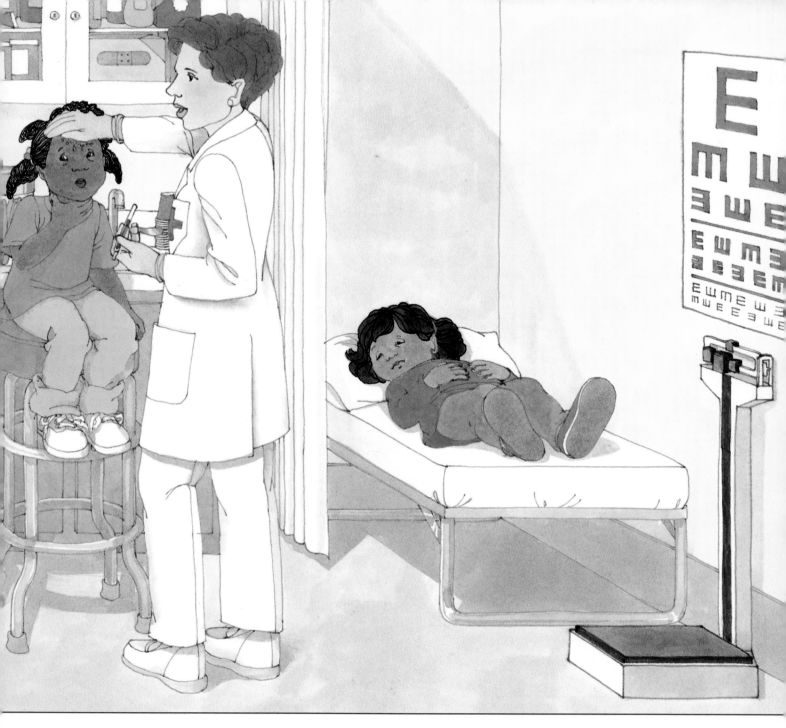

7. blood

8. cut

9. bump

☆10. cough

☆11. sneeze

☆12. lie down

Music!

1. 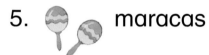 violin

2. trumpet

3. tuba

4. flute

5. maracas

6. piano

7.  bongo drums

8. △ triangle

☆9. blow

☆10.  beat

☆11. clap

☆12. sing

1. police officer

2. traffic

3.  traffic light

4. truck

5. motorcycle

6. taxi

7. police station

8. library

9. sports store

10.  pet shop

11.  barbershop

12.  toy store

Look at the toys!

1. game

2. airplane

3. boat

4. doll

5. animals

6. train

7. money

8. quarter

9. dime

10. nickel

11. penny

12. dollar

Can we have a pet?

1. bird

2. fish

3.  fish tank

4. turtle

5. mouse

6. cage

7. dog

8. cat

9. kitten

10. puppy

11. collar

12. leash

Let's go to the library!

AUTHOR: KEYES, J.R.
TITLE: OUR EARTH
SUBJECT: EARTH SCIENCE
CALL NUMBER: 551 K

1. magazine

2. newspaper

3. atlas

4. dictionary

5. computer

6. call number

7. videotape

8. bookshelves

9. library card

10. due date

☆11. check out

☆12. return

I'm sick!

examination room

1. doctor

2. patient

3. checkup

4. chart

5. scale

6. stethoscope

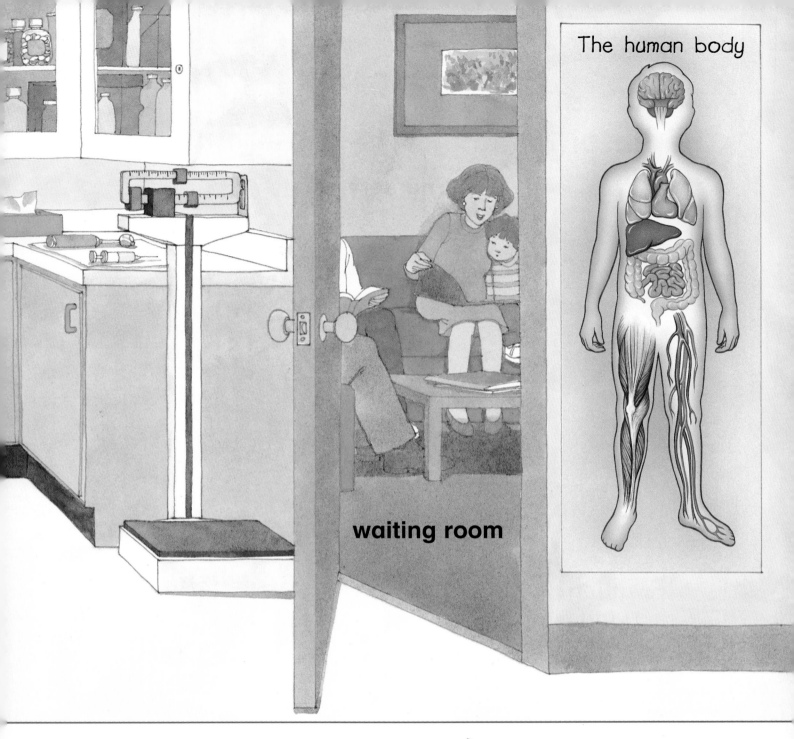

The human body

waiting room

7.	medicine	10.	prescription
8.	drops	11.	tablets
9.	spray	12.	shot

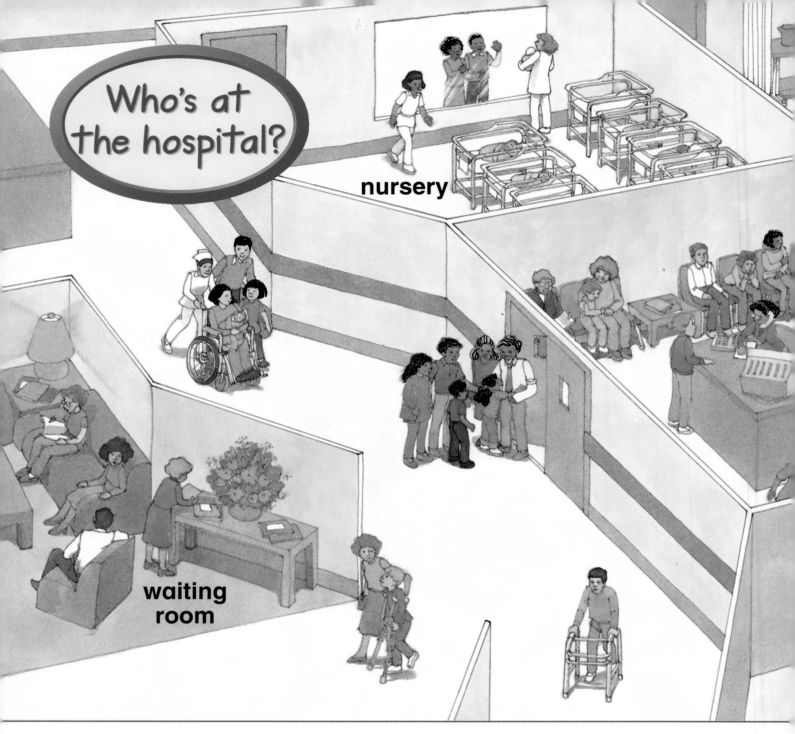

Who's at the hospital?

nursery

waiting room

1.  siren

2.  ambulance

3. paramedic

4. stretcher

5. mask

6. rubber gloves

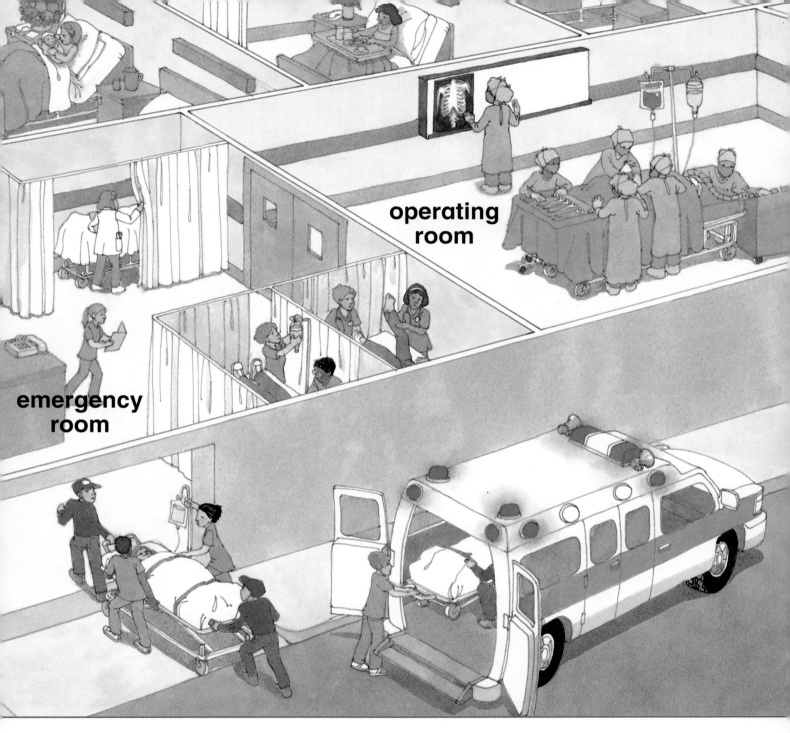

7. X ray

8. wheelchair

9. walker

10. crutches

11. cast

12. blanket

Busy supermarket!

MEAT

SEAFO

1.  list

2. pineapple

3. bananas

4. orange

5. meat

6. seafood

7. box

8. bags

9.  cart

10.  lettuce

11. broccoli

12. cheese

Errands in town

1. restaurant

2. hardware store

3. drugstore

4. letter

5. letter carrier

6. mailbox

7. post office

8. dentist

9. laundry

10. bakery

11. bank

12. gas station

Dinner's ready!

1. **roast beef**

2. **potato**

3.  **peas**

4. **tomato**

5. **rolls**

6. **apple pie**

7. soup

8. corn

9. chicken

10. rice

11. beans

12. melon

Nice evening!

1. stereo

2.  television

3. remote

4. CD

5.  headphones

6. radio

 7. rest

 8. play

9. watch

 10. help

 11. talk

12. practice

Saturday at the mall

1.  movie theater

2. arcade

3. snack bar

4. pizza

5. french fries

6. ice cream cone

7. soda

8. shoe store

9. clothing store

10. rest rooms

11. escalator

12.  exit

1.  balloon

2. present

3. card

4. ribbon

5. wrapping paper

6. baseball bat

January								February						
S	M	T	W	T	F	S	S	M	T	W	T	F	S
						1		1	2	3	4	5	
2	3	4	5	6	7	8	6	7	8	9	10	11	12
9	10	11	12	13	14	15	13	14	15	16	17	18	19
16	17	18	19	20	21	22	20	21	22	23	24	25	26
23	24	25	26	27	28	29	27	28	29				
30	31												

March								April						
S	M	T	W	T	F	S	S	M	T	W	T	F	S
		1	2	3	4								1
5	6	7	8	9	10	11	2	3	4	5	6	7	8
12	13	14	15	16	17	18	9	10	11	12	13	14	15
19	20	21	22	23	24	25	16	17	18	19	20	21	22
26	27	28	29	30	31		23	24	25	26	27	28	29
							30						

May								June						
S	M	T	W	T	F	S	S	M	T	W	T	F	S
	1	2	3	4	5	6					1	2	3
7	8	9	10	11	12	13	4	5	6	7	8	9	10
14	15	16	17	18	19	20	11	12	13	14	15	16	17
21	22	23	24	25	26	27	18	19	20	21	22	23	24
28	29	30	31				25	26	27	28	29	30	

July								August						
S	M	T	W	T	F	S	S	M	T	W	T	F	S
						1		1	2	3	4	5	
2	3	4	5	6	7	8	6	7	8	9	10	11	12
9	10	11	12	13	14	15	13	14	15	16	17	18	19
16	17	18	19	20	21	22	20	21	22	23	24	25	26
23	24	25	26	27	28	29	27	28	29	30	31		
30	31												

September								October						
S	M	T	W	T	F	S	S	M	T	W	T	F	S
					1	2	1	2	3	4	5	6	7
3	4	5	6	7	8	9	8	9	10	11	12	13	14
10	11	12	13	14	15	16	15	16	17	18	19	20	21
17	18	19	20	21	22	23	22	23	24	25	26	27	28
24	25	26	27	28	29	30	29	30	31				

November								December						
S	M	T	W	T	F	S	S	M	T	W	T	F	S
			1	2	3	4						1	2
5	6	7	8	9	10	11	3	4	5	6	7	8	9
12	13	14	15	16	17	18	10	11	12	13	14	15	16
19	20	21	22	23	24	25	17	18	19	20	21	22	23
26	27	28	29	30			24	25	26	27	28	29	30
							31						

7.  jewelry

8. puzzle

9. helicopter

10. candy

11. cake

12. candles

Sunday in
the city

1. airport

2. railroad

3. highway

4. factory

5. smokestack

6. litter

7. street cleaner

8. garbage truck

9. skyscrapers

10. park

11. bench

12. subway

Street scene

1. singer
2. dancer
3. musician

4.  guitar
5. photographer
6. camera

7. theater

8. museum

9. steps

10. mime

11. artist

12. painting

New building going up!

1. backhoe

2. dump truck

3. cement mixer

4. crane

5. forklift

6.  bulldozer

7.  construction worker

8. carpenter

9. plumber

10. electrician

11.  pipe

12. wire

 **Fire!**

1. smoke

2.  flame

3. fire engine

4. firefighter

5. fire chief

6. fire hydrant

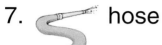 7. hose

8. axe

 9. ladder

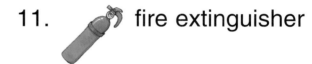 10. air tank

11. fire extinguisher

 12. fire escape

Big harbor

1. sunset

2. lighthouse

3. ship

4. buoy

5. sailboat

6.  bridge

7.  ferry

8. dock

9. barge

10. warehouse

11. tugboat

12. anchor

Carnival!

1. ticket

2. popcorn

3. cotton candy

4. acrobat

5. trapeze

6. costume

7. magician

8. clown

9. Ferris wheel

10.  carousel

11.  puppet show

12.  fireworks

1.  tablecloth

2.  napkin

3. apron

4. pots

5.  chef

6.  menu

7. chopsticks

8. waiter

*9. pour

*10. stir

*11. chop

*12.  serve

Let's see the USA!

1. desert

2. peninsula

3. mountains

4. lake

5. gulf

6. coast

7. forest

8. river

9. wetlands

10. plains

11. glacier

12. island

Beach day

1. seagull

2. sand

3.  wave

4. sunburn

5. sunblock

6. lifeguard

7. surfboard

8. bathing suit

9. kite

☆10. swim

☆11. dive

☆12. float

We found a tide pool!

BIRD SANCTUARY KEEP OUT

1. pail

2.  shovel

3.  stones

4. shells

5.  clams

6.  crabs

7. snail

8. minnows

9. seaweed

10. duck

11. goose / geese

12.  pelican

What's under the sea?

1.  dolphin

2. whale

3. spout

4. fins

5. snorkel

6.  school

7.  coral reef

8. sea horse

9. shark

10.  jellyfish

11. octopus

12. tentacles

Working on the farm

1. farmer

2. barn

3. tractor

4. cow

5. hen

6. rooster

7. sheep

8. pig

☆9.  drive

☆10.  pick

☆11.  feed

☆12.  milk

Camping out

1. sunrise

2. waterfall

3. tent

4. sleeping bag

5. life jacket

6. rowboat

7. fishing rod

8. poison ivy

9. frog

10. deer

11. bear

12. woods

Bugs!

larva

eggs

pupa

adult

1. ant

2. spider

3. web

4. caterpillar

5. cocoon

6. butterfly

7. bee

8. ticks

9. firefly

10. mosquito

11. magnifying glass

12. bug spray

Ranch in the desert

1. cowhand

2. cactus

3. rattlesnake

4. coyote

5. prairie dog

6. lizard

7. horseback riding

8. rocks

9. lasso

10. buffalo

11. scorpion

12. horse

Dinosaur days

1. fossil

2. scientist

3. dinosaurs

4. Oviraptor

5. Pterosaur

6. Triceratops

7. Stegosaurus

8. Tyrannosaurus Rex

9. Diplodocus

10. asteroid

11. volcano

12. lava

Who lives in the zoo?

AUSTRALIAN ANIMALS

ASIAN ANIMALS

1.  peacock

2. monkeys

3. elephant

4. tiger

5. lion

6. snakes

7. ape

8. feathers

9. tail

10. trunk

11. scales

12. fur

I'm in Australia!

1. emu

2. dingo

3. koala

4. kangaroo

5. joey

6. wichity grubs

7. wombat

8. kookaburra

9. parrot

10. claws

11. pouch

12. wings

I'm in Africa!

1. gazelle

2. hippopotamus

3. zebra

4. giraffe

5. gorilla

6. chimpanzee

7.  baboon

8.  flamingo

9. leopard

10. jaws

11. spots

12. stripes

I'm in Asia!

1. camel

2. orangutan

3. crocodile

4. cobra

5. rhinoceros

6. egret

7. panda

8. bamboo

9. humps

10. horn

11. beak

12. fangs

Spring is here!

1. grass

2.  bush

3.  flowers

4. lawn mower

5. rabbit

6. seeds

dig   plant   cover   water

7. robin

8. nest

9. squirrel

10. raccoon

11. hammer

12. saw

We planted a garden!

1. sunshine

2. rain

3. soil

4. seed

5. root

6. sprout

7. stem

8. leaf

9. bud

10. flower

11. raincoat

12. umbrella

Hot summer

1.  pool

2. baseball

3. tennis

4. waterskiing

5. skates

6. picnic

7. hamburger

8.  hot dog

9.  clouds

10.  wind

11. 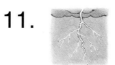 lightning

12.  thunderstorm

Windy fall

1. leaves

2. rake

3. pile

4.  wheelbarrow

5. clippers

6. broom

7. bulbs

8. football

9. soccer

10. pumpkin

11. woodpecker

12. nuts

Snowy winter

1. snow

2. snowflakes

3. snowman

4. snowball

5. icicles

6. sled

7. ice skating

8.  skiing

9.  hat

10.  jacket

11.  gloves

12.  scarf

Up in the night sky

1. moon

2. stars

3. constellation

4. meteor

5. comet

6. planets

7. astronomer

8. telescope

9.  full moon

10. half moon

11. crescent moon

12. new moon

Out in space

Saturn

Jupiter

Neptune

Uranus

Pluto

1. The Sun

2. Mercury

3. Venus

4. Earth

5. Mars

6. Jupiter

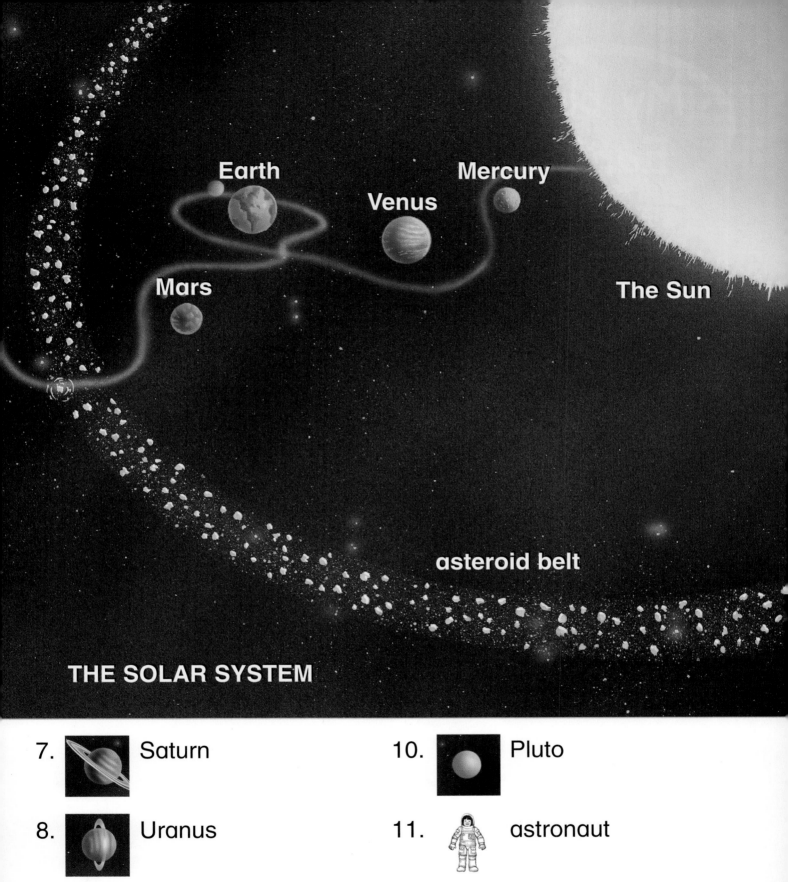

Earth

Mercury

Venus

Mars

The Sun

asteroid belt

THE SOLAR SYSTEM

7. Saturn

8. Uranus

9. Neptune

10. Pluto

11. astronaut

12. spaceship

My blue
Earth

Appendix

The Alphabet

A a　B b　C c

D d　E e　F f

G g　H h　I i

J j　K k　L l

M m　N n　O o

P p   Q q   R r

S s   T t   U u

V v   W w   X x

Y y   Z z

Numbers

1 one ●

2 two ● ●

3 three ● ● ●

4 four ● ● ● ●

5 five ● ● ● ● ●

6 six ● ● ● ● ● ●

7 seven ● ● ● ● ● ● ●

8 eight ● ● ● ● ● ● ● ●

9 nine ● ● ● ● ● ● ● ● ●

10 ten ● ● ● ● ● ● ● ● ● ●

11 eleven ● ● ● ● ● ● ● ● ● ● ●

12 twelve ● ● ● ● ● ● ● ● ● ● ● ●

13 thirteen ● ● ● ● ● ● ● ● ● ● ● ● ●

14 fourteen ● ● ● ● ● ● ● ● ● ● ● ● ● ●

15 fifteen ● ● ● ● ● ● ● ● ● ● ● ● ● ● ●

16 sixteen ● ● ● ● ● ● ● ● ● ● ● ● ● ● ● ●

17 seventeen ● ● ● ● ● ● ● ● ● ● ● ● ● ● ● ● ●

18 eighteen ● ● ● ● ● ● ● ● ● ● ● ● ● ● ● ● ● ●

19 nineteen ● ● ● ● ● ● ● ● ● ● ● ● ● ● ● ● ● ● ●

20 twenty ●

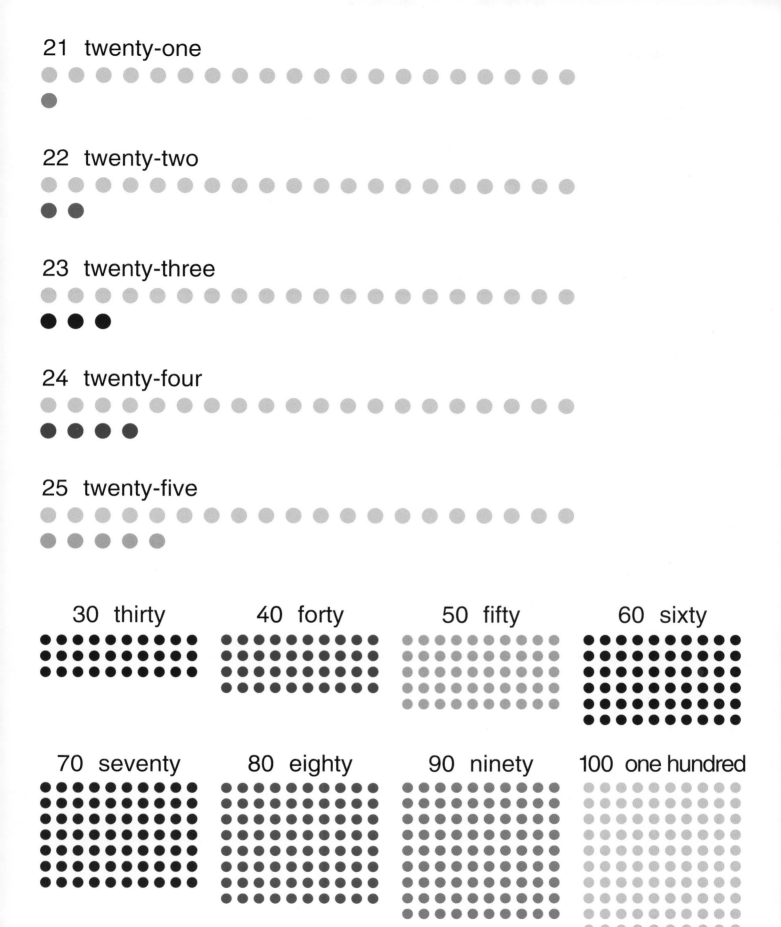

21 twenty-one

22 twenty-two

23 twenty-three

24 twenty-four

25 twenty-five

30 thirty

40 forty

50 fifty

60 sixty

70 seventy

80 eighty

90 ninety

100 one hundred

Ordinal Numbers

1st first ★ ☆ ☆ ☆ ☆ ☆ ☆ ☆ ☆ ☆

2nd second ☆ ★ ☆ ☆ ☆ ☆ ☆ ☆ ☆ ☆

3rd third ☆ ☆ ★ ☆ ☆ ☆ ☆ ☆ ☆ ☆

4th fourth ☆ ☆ ☆ ★ ☆ ☆ ☆ ☆ ☆ ☆

5th fifth ☆ ☆ ☆ ☆ ★ ☆ ☆ ☆ ☆ ☆

6th sixth ☆ ☆ ☆ ☆ ☆ ★ ☆ ☆ ☆ ☆

7th seventh ☆ ☆ ☆ ☆ ☆ ☆ ★ ☆ ☆ ☆

8th eighth ☆ ☆ ☆ ☆ ☆ ☆ ☆ ★ ☆ ☆

9th ninth ☆ ☆ ☆ ☆ ☆ ☆ ☆ ☆ ★ ☆

10th tenth ☆ ☆ ☆ ☆ ☆ ☆ ☆ ☆ ☆ ★

Colors

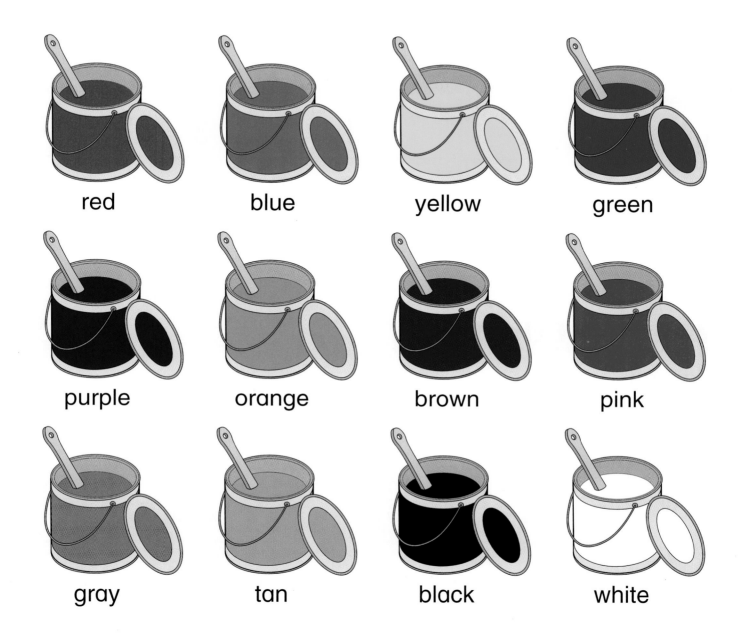

red

blue

yellow

green

purple

orange

brown

pink

gray

tan

black

white

Shapes

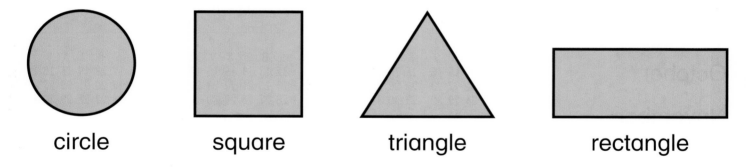

circle

square

triangle

rectangle

Days of the Week

Sunday

Monday

Tuesday

Wednesday

Thursday

Friday

Saturday

Sunday	Monday	Tuesday	Wednesday	Thursday	Friday	Saturday
		1	2	3	4	5
6	7	8	9	10	11	12
13	14	15	16	17	18	19

Months of the Year

January

February

March

April

May

June

July

August

September

October

November

December

January

S	M	T	W	T	F	S
						1
2	3	4	5	6	7	8
9	10	11	12	13	14	15
16	17	18	19	20	21	22
23	24	25	26	27	28	29
30	31					

February

S	M	T	W	T	F	S
		1	2	3	4	5
6	7	8	9	10	11	12
13	14	15	16	17	18	19
20	21	22	23	24	25	26
27	28	29				

March

S	M	T	W	T	F	S
		1	2	3	4	
5	6	7	8	9	10	11
12	13	14	15	16	17	18
19	20	21	22	23	24	25
26	27	28	29	30	31	

April

S	M	T	W	T	F	S
						1
2	3	4	5	6	7	8
9	10	11	12	13	14	15
16	17	18	19	20	21	22
23	24	25	26	27	28	29
30						

May

S	M	T	W	T	F	S
	1	2	3	4	5	6
7	8	9	10	11	12	13
14	15	16	17	18	19	20
21	22	23	24	25	26	27
28	29	30	31			

June

S	M	T	W	T	F	S
				1	2	3
4	5	6	7	8	9	10
11	12	13	14	15	16	17
18	19	20	21	22	23	24
25	26	27	28	29	30	

July

S	M	T	W	T	F	S
						1
2	3	4	5	6	7	8
9	10	11	12	13	14	15
16	17	18	19	20	21	22
23	24	25	26	27	28	29
30	31					

August

S	M	T	W	T	F	S
	1	2	3	4	5	
6	7	8	9	10	11	12
13	14	15	16	17	18	19
20	21	22	23	24	25	26
27	28	29	30	31		

September

S	M	T	W	T	F	S
					1	2
3	4	5	6	7	8	9
10	11	12	13	14	15	16
17	18	19	20	21	22	23
24	25	26	27	28	29	30

October

S	M	T	W	T	F	S
1	2	3	4	5	6	7
8	9	10	11	12	13	14
15	16	17	18	19	20	21
22	23	24	25	26	27	28
29	30	31				

November

S	M	T	W	T	F	S
		1	2	3	4	
5	6	7	8	9	10	11
12	13	14	15	16	17	18
19	20	21	22	23	24	25
26	27	28	29	30		

December

S	M	T	W	T	F	S
					1	2
3	4	5	6	7	8	9
10	11	12	13	14	15	16
17	18	19	20	21	22	23
24	25	26	27	28	29	30
31						

Time

5:00

5 pm

five o'clock

5:15

five fifteen

a quarter past five

5:30

five thirty

half past five

5:45

five forty-five

a quarter to six

Words

Words shown in red are in illustrations only. Words in black are in illustrations and text.

Verbs

Topic 6: Good morning!
brush
cook
eat
get dressed
sleep
wash

Topic 10: Here comes the school bus!
lean
push
sit
stand

Topic 11: Time for school!
ride
walk

Topic 12: What are you making?
build
cut
listen
look
paint

Topic 13: Where's my homework?
draw
read
think
write

Topic 15: What's new in the hall?
cry
frown
laugh
smile
yawn

Topic 16: Gym time!
crawl
hop
jump
skip
tumble

Topic 18: Let's play!
bounce
catch
climb
fall
kick
run
throw

Topic 19: What's the matter?
cough
lie down
sneeze

Topic 20: Music!
beat
blow
clap
sing

Topic 24: Let's go to the library!
check out
return

Topic 30: Nice evening!
help
play
practice
rest
talk
watch

Topic 39: Great restaurant!
chop
pour
serve
stir

Topic 41: Beach day
dive
float
swim

Topic 44: Working on the farm
drive
feed
milk
pick

Subjects

Animals

Topic 23: Can we have a pet?
bird
cat
dog
fish
kitten
mouse
puppy
turtle

Topic 41: Beach day
seagull

Topic 42: We found a tide pool!
clams
crabs
duck
geese
goose
minnows
pelican
snail

Topic 43: What's under the sea?
dolphin
jellyfish
octopus
sea horse
shark
whale

Topic 44: Working on the farm
cow
hen
pig
rooster
sheep

Topic 45: Camping out
bear
deer
frog

Topic 46: Bugs!
ant
bee
butterfly
caterpillar
firefly
mosquito
spider
tick

Topic 47: Ranch in the desert
buffalo
coyote
horse
lizard

prairie dog
rattlesnake
scorpion

Topic 48: Dinosaur days
dinosaurs
Diplodocus
Oviraptor
Pterosaur
Stegosaurus
Triceratops
Tyrannosaurus Rex

Topic 49: Who lives in the zoo?
apes
elephant
lion
monkeys
peacock
snakes
tiger

Topic 50: I'm in Australia!
dingo
emu
joey
kangaroo
koala
kookaburra
parrot
wichity grubs
wombat

Topic 51: I'm in Africa!
baboon
chimpanzee
flamingo
gazelle
giraffe
gorilla
hippopotamus
leopard
zebra

Topic 52: I'm in Asia!
camel
cobra
crocodile
egret
orangutan
panda
rhinoceros

Topic 53: Spring is here!
rabbit
raccoon
robin
squirrel

Topic 56: Windy fall
woodpecker

Body

Topic 3: Different faces
- chin
- ears
- eyelashes
- eyes
- hair
- mouth
- nose
- skin
- teeth
- tooth

Topic 14: Bodies and bones!
- ankle
- arm
- back
- buttocks
- chest
- elbow
- feet
- fingers
- foot
- hand
- head
- hip
- knee
- leg
- neck
- ribs
- shoulder
- skull
- stomach
- spine
- toes
- wrist

Clothing

Topic 8: What can I wear?
- baseball cap
- boots
- dress
- jeans
- pajamas
- skirt
- sneakers
- socks
- sweater
- sweatshirt
- T-shirt
- underwear

Topic 26: Who's at the hospital?
- mask
- rubber gloves

Topic 38: Carnival!
- costume

Topic 41: Beach day
- bathing suit

Topic 45: Camping out
- life jacket

Topic 54: We planted a garden!
- raincoat

Topic 57: Snowy winter
- gloves
- hat
- jacket
- scarf

Food

Topic 9: Who made breakfast?
- bread
- butter
- cereal
- eggs
- juice

Topic 17: What's for lunch?
- apple
- carrot
- cookie
- egg roll
- milk
- salad
- sandwich
- sushi
- taco

Topic 27: Busy supermarket!
- bananas
- broccoli
- cheese
- lettuce
- meat
- orange
- pineapple
- seafood

Topic 29: Dinner's ready
- apple pie
- beans
- chicken
- corn
- melon
- peas
- potato
- rice
- roast beef
- rolls
- soup
- tomato

Topic 31: Saturday at the mall
- french fries
- ice cream cone
- pizza
- soda

Topic 32: Happy birthday!
- cake
- candy

Topic 38: Carnival!
- cotton candy
- popcorn

Topic 55: Hot summer
- hamburger
- hot dog

Neighborhood Places

Topic 5: Where do you live?
- apartment
- house
- street
- yard

Topic 10: Here comes the school bus!
- bus stop
- corner

Topic 18: Let's play!
- bars
- seesaw
- slide
- swing

Topic 33: Sunday in the city
- park

Occupations

Topic 10: Here comes the school bus!
- bus driver

Topic 11: Time for school
- crossing guard
- librarian
- nurse
- principal
- student
- teacher

Topic 21: Can we cross now?
- police officer

Topic 25: I'm sick!
- doctor

Topic 26: Who's at the hospital?
- paramedic

Topic 28: Errands in town
- dentist
- letter carrier

Topic 34: Street scene
- artist
- dancer
- mime
- musician
- photographer
- singer

Topic 35: New building going up!
- carpenter
- construction worker
- electrician
- plumber

Topic 36: Fire!
- fire chief
- firefighter

Topic 38: Carnival!
- acrobat
- clown
- magician

Topic 39: Great restaurant!
- chef
- waiter

Topic 41: Beach day
- lifeguard

Topic 44: Working on the farm
- farmer

Topic 47: Ranch in the desert
- cowhand

Topic 48: Dinosaur days
- scientist

Topic 58: Up in the night sky
- astronomer

Topic 59: Out in space
- astronaut

Sport And Physical Activity

Topic 18: Let's play!
- ball
- bars
- bounce
- catch
- climb
- kick
- run
- seesaw
- slide
- swing
- throw

Topic 32: Happy birthday!
- baseball bat

Topic 37: Big harbor
- sailboat

Topic 41: Beach day
- dive
- float

The Oxford Picture Dictionary for Kids

Dictionaries

Components

Kids' Readers

Readers Components